DAILY P DIVIN

GW01191215

A SHORT INTRODUCTION

JOHN-FRANCIS FRIENDSHIP

DARTON · LONGMAN + TODD

First published in 2023 by
Darton, Longman and Todd Ltd
1 Spencer Court
140 – 142 Wandsworth High Street
London SW18 4JJ

ISBN: 978-1-915412-54-6

A catalogue record for this book is available from
the British Library.

Printed and bound in Great Britain
by Bell & Bain, Glasgow

Contents

INTRODUCTION

Bless the Lord, you priests of the Lord;
sing praise to him and highly exalt him for ever.
Bless the Lord, you servants of the Lord;
sing praise to him and highly exalt him for ever.
(Song of the Three, v.62f)

༄

THE *DAILY OFFICE* (or *Divine Office, Office of the Hours, Opus Dei*) comprises a structured series of age-old scriptural services marking the passage of time. Offered at least morning and evening there are seven 'Hours' in total, and whilst most people don't celebrate them all some will also pray them, for example, at lunchtime or before going to bed. This call to pray at certain times was adopted by Muslims (*salat*) from the practice of the early church, and the shape and bodily actions (bowing, prostrating, etc.) of each *salah* reflect the prayer of those first Christians.

Because the Office now appears in a variety of versions this booklet is based on a generic format with the intention that readers might discover the benefits of these aids to prayer, deepen their understanding and assist devotion. Some find the Office wordy and cumbersome but that can be the result of historical additions to, quite simply, a prayerful engagement with the psalms and other scriptures which can be traced back to worship in the Jerusalem Temple.

Composed of mainly biblical material it is, first and foremost, a response to the command to 'love the Lord your God with all your heart, and with all your soul, and with all your mind' (Deuteronomy 4:6f.), and because love needs to be the lifeblood of every Christian so it is to be the motivation of worship. Whilst the Office may lack that emotionalism present in some forms of 'modern' worship, that doesn't mean celebrating it without feeling, rather it is to be an offering of the mind in the heart – the centre of our being – expressed by the lips.

It was developed by the Desert Elders – those monks and nuns whom God called into the wilderness places of Egypt, Palestine and Syria – who were moved to join that great chorus of prayer and praise continually offered by creation (cf. Psalm 148). And because St Paul agreed and taught that we are to 'pray without ceasing' (1 Thessalonians 5:17) the Elders set aside times throughout the day which would express what they desired for the whole day. Such an understanding can help those who see 'going to church' as important because what matters is the worship we offer to and through Christ as part of our desire for our lives to reveal his.

Like others I've prayed it in various forms, as layman and priest, for more than half a century. But it was the years I lived as a Religious (Franciscan) that enabled me to realise something of its true riches, and this book is the fruit of that experience. So I've drawn on insights from that Life (explored more fully in *What Do You Seek? Wisdom from Religious Life for Today's World*) because the church has much to learn from those for whom the Office has been the focus of life for almost two thousand years. Whilst most Religious (and clergy) have an obligation to pray them, lay people are also encouraged to join in this Prayer for it is the offering of the whole Church, the Body of Christ, which constantly prays to the Father (Hebrews 7:25).

My first experience of it was Sunday Evensong from the 1662 Book of Common Prayer (BCP) at my Anglican parish church. I was in my mid-teens and, later, tried Matins but found myself wondering why the priest intoned 'O Lord, open thou our lips' at 11 a.m. as if those were the first words spoken that day (which they are meant to be). But it was in joining with the (Anglican) sisters of the Community of St Mary the Virgin (CSMV) in celebrating plainsong Vespers (Evensong) at their convent in Wantage in Berkshire, UK, that I discovered this treasury of prayer and praise provides a way of entering that great river of worship that has flowed for millennia. I sensed it opened 'the gateway to the vision of God for which we were created'[1] and isn't dependent on mood, ability, or experience.

Many would agree with Dom John Chapman OSB (1865-1933) who says in his *Spiritual Letters*: 'Pray as you can, and do not try to pray as you can't' (109), but that can lead to believing real prayer can *only* be spontaneous, which runs the risk of preventing our prayer-life developing. But Christians have always valued using ways others have found helpful and the psalms (and hymns) are a clear example of this. Using them involves a certain humility as we allow ourselves to be guided by their words. They can lead us into the mysteries of the Passion, Death and Resurrection of Christ, foreshadowed throughout the Hebrew scriptures, and it is through that prism – the Heart of Christ – we are to pray them.

THE PSALMS

O amazing wonder! Many who have made little progress in Literature know the Psalter by heart. Nor is it only in cities and churches that David is famous; in the village market, in the desert, and in uninhabitable land, he excites the praise of God. In monasteries, among those holy choirs of angelic armies, David is first, last and central. In the convents of virgins, communities of those who imitate Mary; in the deserts where there are men crucified to the world, who live their life in heaven with God, David is first, last, and central.

(*St John Chrysostom*, d. 407 AD) [2]

TODAY IN MOST churches – let alone in daily conversation – the Psalms are hardly 'first, last and central'. Yet they were fundamental to the prayer of early Christians, just as they are important for Jews, and the Office developed as a vehicle for praying them. They formed the bulk of most Offices and, as part of the wisdom tradition, were understood to express the depths of creation's (of which we're part) relationship with the Creator. The words speak into the heart as they are constantly repeated, expressing the desire to be recreated by God. They inform the heart of the one who prays them and, gradually, refashion it.

Part of their power lies in the way they draw on metaphor, myth and imagery to enable a deepening of prayer, whilst expressing every emotion and the whole of life's complexities and contradictions. Their repetition bathes the heart in that wisdom which comes from above. Yet praying them *can* begin to feel monotonous, which is why it's important to remember our need for recollection – that constant returning of the heart's eye and mind to God. As prayer, which St Teresa of Avila compared with being on terms of friendship with God, they aid us in developing an undivided heart enfolding the mind's desire for the divine (e.g. Psalm 62).

Early Christians realised the Psalms had helped express Jesus' relationship with the Father and, by repeating them, they were immersing themselves in words he chanted. Dietrich Bonhoeffer, the German pastor and writer murdered at Auschwitz in 1945, subtitled his work on them: '*The Prayer Book of the Bible*'; they remind us that we are sinners seeking a Saviour, not least when they cry out for mercy, placing us in that dynamic by which the Creator deals with creation and enabling our soul to sing with joy as we see God at work. This is of particular importance as it provides the 'bridge' between praying them and experiencing God in all things. This can be of especial importance when the heart may feel a certain emptiness, for we need to recall that, like the psalmist, we are to relish and give thanks for the presence of God in all creation.

> You send forth your spirit, and they are created,*
> and so you renew the face of the earth.
> May the glory of the LORD endure forever!*
> May the LORD rejoice in all his works!
> (Psalm 104:30f.)

The 'poetic-parallel' shown above with which many psalms were written also aids their appeal:

> I said, 'I will keep watch over my ways, *
> so that I do not offend with my tongue.
> (Psalm 39:1)

the second half mirroring, from a slightly different angle, what the psalmist sought to express in the preceding half. This 'parallelism' takes various forms, often opening the subject through further reflection:

O Lord I am not proud;*
I have no haughty looks.

(Psalm 131:1)

the final line of the verse leading into the reflection of the next:

I do not occupy myself with great matters,*
or with things that are too hard for me.

(Psalm 131:2)

St Benedict (480-547 AD), in his *Rule*, said: 'let the mind be in harmony with the voice' (Ch. 19), an understanding he may have discovered from earlier sources. St Cyprian of Carthage (d. 258 AD) wrote: 'God does not hearken to the voice, but to the heart.' More recently someone has also observed that: 'If the heart doesn't pray, the tongue only plays.'

Like all prayers, the psalms are not to be rushed but savoured. They should be said (or sung) in a measured manner with a definite pause (approximately three seconds) during the verse to enable a reflective pace. This also permits the words to enter the heart before praying the next line and is especially helpful in allowing the echo of the poetic-parallel to descend into the silence.

When prayed with others, verses can be

shared by alternate groups or by one person whilst others respond with a refrain (antiphon) expressing something of the essence of the psalm season or Feast. None should dominate; all need to be conscious of being part of a body praying with a single heart and voice. It is, therefore, an exercise in humble, contemplative listening as we hear others rather than ourselves. For similar reasons, and to avoid expressing feelings others may not share, we shouldn't emphasise any particular word or phrase. (I still recall a dear, elderly Religious who always prayed: 'Glory be to the Father, *and* to the Son, **and** to the … ', as if to make sure none of the Trinity felt ignored.)

THE WORD AND WORDS

But a note of caution: avoid being trapped by words. We might feel like saying: 'Lord, how many adversaries I have' (Psalm 3:1), but the psalmist prevents us from dwelling on any desire for vengeance by quickly affirming: 'Deliverance belongs to the Lord' (v. 8). Yet they do give permission to pray what we might not feel able to articulate: 'declare them guilty, O God; let them fall, because of their schemes' (5:11), whilst recognising that we need to pray 'have pity on me, Lord for I am weak; heal me, Lord, for my bones are racked' (6:2).

What, then, of those 'cursing psalms', or

verses (often bracketed in the text) expressing aggressive emotions? Many prefer to omit them – probably sensible in public worship – but others think they allow us to own humbly, before God, our negativity.

USE OF THE PSALMS

They provide a perfect, rhythmic way of meditating on God's mysteries. In whatever way the Psalms are offered there's opportunity to be present to the words as they are uttered, letting what is expressed with the lips be inbreathed into the heart. Yet whilst we're to be present to what the psalmist sought to convey, we also need to allow them to open *us* to what the Spirit seeks to communicate *now*.

There are many ways in which they can be used, different books suggesting various methods, but it's possible to recognise a beneficial pattern throughout. The authors, of which there were a number, expressed a love for God which is the basis of all worship and prayer (Psalm 18:1f.). Realising their sinfulness, they beg forgiveness (Psalm 38); having found freedom through this gift of God they entrust themselves to God's mercy (Psalm 51) and, acknowledging God's glory, offer that thanks and praise (Psalm 100) which enfolds all created things (Psalm 139).

The psalmist's awareness of God in creation is

reflected by saints like Cuthbert of Iona (AD 634 - 687), Francis of Assisi (1181/2-1226), Silouan the Athonite (1866-1938) and, most perceptively, Bonaventure (1221-1274), seventh Franciscan Minister General. Their insights informed my understanding of the Psalms, opening my heart's eye to the way creation glows with the presence of the Creator. Each mountain and hill, the oceans, rivers, earth and stars move me as I gaze upon them. That may sound odd to some twenty-first century Western ears but our forebears knew they were profoundly connected with the rest of the created order, something we're – slowly – beginning to realise again. After all, we are of the stuff of which stars are made.

Aware of nature's sacredness I find myself, like some elderly hippy, prayerfully touching an ancient oak tree I pass on local walks. I understood Bonaventure's assertion that 'Creation is like a beautiful song that flows in the most excellent of harmonies, but it is a song that God *freely* desires to sing into the vast spaces of the universe. There's nothing that compels God to chant the hymn of the universe. Creation is simply the sacred outflow of a loving God in whose infinite, dynamic goodness we share. Creation is God's "other".' [3]

That helps me understand why my heart is uplifted, and why it laments when nature is abused. Many psalms also prevent us from dwelling too long on any negative feelings that can lead to neurosis, or feed the ego – 'he's always attacking me, so … '; left to ourselves, prayer can become fixated in unhealthy ways. Even when expressing depths of fear, terror, loneliness and pain they reach a point where we must trustfully let go of whatever might have caught our attention. They lead us to realise and admit the wonders of God's dealings with creation, re-awakening us to what our ancestors knew: 'The heavens declare the glory of God, and the firmament shows his handiwork' (Psalm 19:1f.).

This constant affirmation of the good purposes of God reinforces the foundation of faith: 'those who know your name will put their trust in you, for you never forsake those who seek you, O Lord. Sing praise to the Lord who dwells in Sion, proclaim to the peoples the things he has done' (Psalm 9:10f). In this way we're drawn into those fundamental virtues of faith, hope, and love. Finally, they affirm our place with angels and saints in the whole created order (Psalm 148:1-5).

All psalms were written for singing (cf. Ezra 3:11) to simple, plainsong-like melodies created to resonate in the soul, music which connects with its movements. Singing psalms (and canticles), even on one note, is an aid to prayer for, as Augustine affirmed: 'he who sings praise, does not only praise, but also praises joyously; he who sings praise, is not only singing, but also loving Him whom he is singing about/to/for.[4] Or, more popularly: 'Whoever sings well (i.e. with sincerity and love), prays twice'. So, if you pray alone, sing (or say) them aloud and be carried by the voice of psalmist – let his words enfold you. What is written is all about human thriving through utter dependency on God. Pray in a recollected way, let the words seep into you and feed on them; let go of distractions – and take a similar approach with the scriptures.

'LEVELS' OF PRAYER

There are at least three levels at which the Psalms can be prayed:

- *Ground floor* – aware of the words and 'chewing' on them, letting them carry us through the narrative.
- *Basement* – being carried into the depths by the words, sinking beneath them.
- *Roof top* – allowing them to 'launch' us into the Divine Mystery.

Francis of Assisi was so moved by the Psalms that he not only directed they should be used by his brothers (and members of the Third Order) but also developed his own versions to praise God's saving activity, not least in creation:

Let heaven and earth praise him who is glorious
Let us praise and glorify him above all forever.

And every creature that is in heaven
and on earth and under earth
and in the sea and those which are in them.
Let us praise and glorify him above all forever.

He called it the *Little Office of the Passion of the Lord*, drawing on the Psalms to express joy and gladness, sorrow, wonder, penitence and praise to aid awareness of God's goodness and mercy.

THE
SPIRITUALITY OF
THE OFFICE

'The ascending life of worship to which men *(sic)* are invited is destined to become at last a life of charity. … Thus worship in all its degrees is an education in love, a purgation of egoism. As it draws nearer to God, Divine Light will itself effect that purification.'[5]

As WITH ALL forms of liturgy (official forms of church worship) the principal purpose of the Office is to unite us with God as we express our love and self-offering. Yet praying it is less about what *we* do and more about what we want God to do with us for, as with any prayer, what we offer unites us with the work of the Holy Spirit (Romans 8:26f.). Its opening plea – 'O God, make speed to save me' (Psalm 70:1) and the following *Gloria* places us in the heart of the Trinity whom we desire to glorify through our offering of mind *and* heart.

Some speak of feeling bored as they pray with so many words, but by allowing them to enter the heart they can enliven us as they become present to us. Remember that we're to let the Word, Jesus, pray in us as he prayed the Psalms; we're one with the whole company of saints in heaven and believers throughout the world, incorporated in the Body of Christ's offering of prayer to the Father.

Our prayer is to be an expression of that Love eternally flowing from the Father through the Son in the power of the Spirit into which we're united. Here we find the source of that stream of Love in which we are to live and move and have our being (Acts 17:28, *cf.* Jeremiah 2:13). Those in the process of Faith formation need teaching about the importance of prayer just as novice Religious and Ordinands might need teaching about the necessity of praying the Office with loving recollection (mindfully – *heart*fully). This is particularly true of the Psalms which are able to speak into the heart (just as all scripture can). Let the words descend into that place and touch you, awakening what they seek to convey:

Bless the LORD, O my soul!
O LORD my God, how great you are,
clothed in majesty and honour,
wrapped in light as with a robe!
(Psalm 104:1f. *Revised Grail*)

20

In this way the Word of the Lord can touch us and aid our prayer, not least when it begins to become dry. By now it might be obvious that praying the Office is an act of godly work – hence, in his Rule for monks, St. Benedict calls it the *opus dei*, a term which could also mean that, through this prayer, God works in us. For prayer, in the end, is not about helping us feel better: it's an aspect of the work of the Holy Spirit who seeks to reconcile all things in God.

PRAYER AND FEELINGS

Whilst most of us can't spend hours in prayer we can benefit from considering how:

> 'Prayer and praise constitute the atmosphere in which (Franciscans) must strive to live … An ever-deepening devotion to Christ is the hidden source of all their strength and joy.'
> (Society of St Francis, *Principles*, Day 14)

The Office has an objectivity that doesn't depend on feelings. A time must come in our life of prayer when God withdraws any 'felt' awareness of the divine Presence so we can learn to desire God for Godself alone and not what we can get from that encounter.

One other thing. I realised in community that any who, in charity, spend much time in regular, formal prayer can notice a deep sense of belonging building up through a growing awareness of others. Although not engaged in conversation a sensitivity developed, something aided by the silence that was part of our common life. Gradually I became conscious of what might be occurring in another's heart which, whilst it's not possible in every church, is a reminder that: 'you are the body of Christ and individually members of it' (1 Corinthians 1:27).

'As thy Infinite Love is ever streaming blessings
     on me,
O let my soul be ever breathing love to thee.'
(Bp. Thomas Ken, *The Practice of Divine Love*,
1685)

THE OFFICE AND THE BODY

Whether on our own or corporately it's best to prepare with a time of silence and stilling of heart and mind. Knowing that silence assists God's presence, enter the church (or wherever) quietly and avoid (noisy) conversations. Sit down, breathe gently, centre yourself into the love of God, for our body aids (or hinders) prayer. Because liturgical prayer is intended to join us with the saints in heaven, standing (when possible) is the ancient Christian attitude (cf. Revelation 7:9f.), whilst sitting is more appropriate for attentive listening – or meditation.

The small cross marked with the tip of the thumb over our lips and that traced by our fingers over the body, bowing from the waist at the *Gloria*; all such outward acts affirm and assist our desire. Even when not prayed with others the Office is best spoken aloud to aid awareness of being united with the whole Church.

COMMON PRAYER

Liturgical prayer has been described as 'the summit towards which *all* the activity of the Church is directed, and the source from which all her power flows'.[6] Praying (not 'saying') the Office requires recollection in order to be as fully present to God as possible. We must never rush, nor can it be a matter of 'me and my prayer'. This is an activity whereby we join with the whole company of saints, living and departed, in their offering to the glory of God and the good of creation. The Holy Spirit is seeking to bind all in bonds of love; we are to be one with Christ whose Heart is given to the Father in perfect harmony within the Trinity, a union which the holy ones praise in song (Revelations 5:8f.).

SINGING

Recalling Vespers with those Wantage Sisters, I remember how deeply I was moved by their plainsong, for which they were famous. In ancient or modern settings Religious know (for they've been singing the Office since the time of the Desert Elders) that it has a particular ability to aid recollected prayer – which is why it was developed. The fact that secular broadcasters and producers of meditation CDs choose it indicates that it continues to connect with our deepest, spiritual nature. When adopted for church congregations it enables the psalms to be prayerfully sung by the people – but if sung by a choir alone we need to listen with deep devotion.

COMMON PRAYER – ITS DEVELOPMENT

THE OFFICE JOINS us in a current of prayer flowing through the world and down the ages. We're praying to 'our' Father and it's 'our' lips that need to open in praise. At the time of Jesus, the Temple had long been regarded as God's dwelling place, the focus of the outpouring of the Divine energies. Some notice the apparent lack of speech, hymn, and psalms in early Temple worship and suggest this reflected a conscious effort to distance the ritual worship of Yahweh from neighbouring deities. It's been said that the priests responsible emphasised the Tabernacle (and, later, the Temple) as a 'sanctuary of silence'[7], a place – primarily – of sacrificial *actions*. Others notice something different: 'Turn to the prayer of your servant and to his supplication, Yahweh my God, to hear the cry and the prayer which your servant prays before you this day' (1 Kings 8:28-30).

Evidence of such worship is offered through

the *Dead Sea Scrolls*. The *Songs of the Sabbath*, poems representing the chants of the angels in heaven, were offered on the first thirteen Sabbaths of the year to accompany the sacrifices thereby implying 'the simultaneity of heavenly and earthly worship.'[8]

> [David] placed singers before the altar,
> to make sweet melody with their voices.
> He gave beauty to the festivals,
> and arranged their times throughout the year,
> while they praised God's holy name,
> And the sanctuary resounded from early
> morning.
>
> (*Hymns for Prayer and Praise*, 247)

They also show how the choice of psalms and canticles became regulated thus enabling worshippers, through the course of the year, to be focussed into the ways God dealt with the world. Jewish liturgical life included the practice of formal prayer at set hours (hence, the 'Hours') which reflected what was happening at that time, uniting everyday life with God's activity.

> 'An individual member who prays is entering an ancient cycle of prayer by which the Church, in the name of the whole creation,

is adoring and praying to the eternal God.'

> (*Evelyn Underhill*, 1875-1941,
> source unknown)

There's clear evidence that Temple worship was understood to relate to the cycle of creation, its liturgies uniting heaven and earth, an understanding revealed through the psalms and today's Office hymns:

> O boundless Wisdom, God most high,
> Creator of the earth and sky,
> With rushing streams and glistening rain
> All living creatures you sustain.
>
> (*Hymns for Prayer and Praise*, 247)

JESUS AND COMMON PRAYER

We don't hear much about the way Jesus joined in worship but, as a devout Jew, we know he shared in both Temple and synagogue services. That involved chanting the Hebrew scriptures (the 'Old Testament'), the offering of psalms and formal liturgies, so in celebrating the Office we're uniting ourselves in a very particular way with Jesus' prayer. Apart from his knowledge of the scriptures it's clear he had memorised psalms (e.g. Psalm 22, *cf.* Matthew 27:46) and may have known all by heart. We might, then, consider that in using them we're 'praying his prayer' and, just as it was for Christ, so this immersion helps us to realise our vocation.

EARLY CHRISTIANS, AND COMMON PRAYER – EUCHARIST AND OFFICE

We also know that the early disciples 'devoted themselves to the apostles' teaching and fellowship, to the breaking of bread and the prayers', spending time in the Temple each day (Acts 2:42f.). We can assume, therefore, that they adopted this practice of praying the psalms at the 'Hours'.

After the Temple's destruction (70 AD), Jewish Christians continued attending synagogue services until approximately 85 AD. We know they also met separately on the eve of the first day of the week, praying overnight and celebrating the Eucharist to unite themselves with Jesus' resurrection. From earliest times that, and what became the Office, were intimately connected for both make Christ present. They concern his lived sacrifice (of prayer and praise) in which we join, and which is fundamental to (Christian) life (Hebrews 13:15). The Roman Preface to Eucharistic Prayer IV makes clear that both concern 'our duty and our salvation ... always and everywhere to give you thanks, Lord, holy Father, almighty and eternal God:

For, although you have no need of our praise,
yet our thanksgiving is itself your gift,
since our praises add nothing to your greatness,
but profit us for salvation …

However, whilst the Eucharist is a corporate celebration, the Office is often a solitary offering, yet aided by unseen hosts of angels and saints. It's part of that great sacrifice offered through, with and in Christ which feeds 'eucharistic living' by which, over time, we deepen our incorporation in him.

MONASTIC GROWTH

As something like an Office began emerging it became of such importance that it is the concern of about twenty out of the seventy-three chapters of St Benedict's *Rule*. Today's 'major' Offices of Morning and Evening Prayer constitute only two of the traditional daytime ones, the others being Terce, Sext, None and Compline. Together with the later addition of Prime, the first of the daylight Hours abandoned by the Roman Catholic Church in the 1970s (although still said by some), they fulfil the biblical injunction: 'seven times a day do I praise you' (Psalm 119:164). The Night Office of Matins/ Nocturns/Vigils or Readings (named for the amount of scripture and other texts used) is still celebrated by some monastics and parts of all these were incorporated into Anglican Matins and Evensong at the Reformation.

COMMON PRAYER – LATER DEVELOPMENTS

The Office uniquely enables the prayer of Temple and synagogue to continue forming us whilst allowing prayer in and with Christ our Messianic Prophet and Great High Priest. It lets the Word, present in the scriptures, have a place in our formation helping to shape us into creatures who, through penitence and praise, are meant to reflect our Creator. Its words are to echo in the heart which is our 'Temple' (1 Corinthians 6:19), the locus of ceaseless praise, prayer and sacrifice.

Whilst God particularly calls Religious to focus their lives into this it is the way for *all* Christians. For our primary call is into the daily conversion of the heart to Christ, and the Office – no matter how frequently celebrated – helps develop a balanced expression of our Faith. For that reason, a 'cathedral' Office emerged early on which, whilst similar to the monastic, was more appropriate for the laity.

Moving on. St Ignatius Loyola (1491-1556) reminded us of the purpose of our humanity at the beginning of his *Spiritual Exercises*: 'Man was created to praise, reverence, and serve God our

Lord and in this way to save his soul' (*Principle and Foundation*). Some notice that Jesuits (Ignatius's brethren) aren't required to celebrate the Office but this isn't through laziness but consequent to a papal dispensation from being tied to whatever might impede their apostolic works – even the Office. Yet many Jesuits pray them privately.

Others may think that 'free-spirited' folk, like Francis of Assisi, needn't be concerned with 'formal' prayers. Yet his writings reveal a love for the seven-fold Office and he even ruled that if brothers couldn't read or had no breviary (a single volume Office book) they should pray a set number of Our Fathers in place of each Hour (something he also applied to the Third Order in the *Rule* of 1221):

'In this as in all things Francis gave the most splendid example. He chanted the psalms with such interior recollection as if he beheld God present. Although he suffered from illness of his eyes, his stomach, his kidneys and his liver, he would not lean on anything while reciting the Office, but prayed in an upright position, with his hood thrown back, never allowing his eyes to wander, or interrupting in any way. If he happened to be on a journey, he would make a stop; if in the saddle, he would dismount. Even when the rain poured down upon him, he would not depart from this custom.'[9]

It was the early Franciscans who popularised the breviary because they could carry it as they walked the roads. They realised it offered a means of articulating the world's praise, taking them into the timeless activity of the Holy Spirit throughout creation both *macro*, as we're taken into the praise of all creation and *micro*, as we're encouraged to open ourselves to that universal activity. This is of such importance that *The Daily Office SSF* points out (1991, p. 677):

> '... (the Office) is part of that praise that the whole creation, consciously or unconsciously, offers to its Creator. Through baptism, each Christian becomes part of that royal priesthood of believers able both to proclaim the word of God and in faith and action to respond to it thereby giving voice to all creation in its ceaseless praise and glory of the eternal creator the source of all its being and life.'

PRAYING THE OFFICE

THE OFFICE SHOULD 'pray us', carry us by its rhythms and movements. If offered with others, it needs to be said slowly and gently with pauses as psalms and canticles are recited or sung. Being recollected in prayer requires that grace of humility as we seek to keep pace with one another. It nurtures awareness whilst offering the means to hear our inner critical, chaotic, judgemental voices and, hearing, repent. This is an aspect of the way to attaining that purity of heart Christ said would enable the vision of God (Matthew 5:8). Called to be present to the Presence through Word and silence it is an expression of the 'Sacrament of the Present Moment' where God is, in and through every aspect of what we say and do.

The daily four-fold Office I prayed for 25 years led me to realise that just as prayer is not dependent on feelings, neither is it to be celebrated only when 'in role'. It offers fruits to be continually relished as words sink into our unconscious for 'the unreflective life is not worth living' (*pace* Socrates). Before Morning, Midday and Evening Prayer Franciscans, like others, say or sing the *Angelus* (*Regina coeli* in Eastertide), that three-fold meditation on the Incarnation/Resurrection. Its origins may lie in Francis' hearing the Islamic call to prayer whilst in the Holy Land and wanting Christians to adopt a similar means to mark times for daily prayer.

Whilst praying the Office is part of the means whereby the world is being reconciled with God, each Hour can also be used as an act of intercession. Many find the following act of recollection of help to praying the Office:

Before the first Hour:
Lord God, I offer this Divine Office to you, together with the adoration and praise of the angels and saints, as well as that of all Religious, those consecrated to lives of prayer and every minister, together with all the devout faithful. Joining my prayer with the prayers of holy Mary the God-bearer, I present to you this chorus of prayer, made holy in the Heart of Jesus, and made one with his most holy prayer.

It's a reminder of how our prayer needs to be one

with Christ's which, ascending with the praise of the angelic host, is made in the heart of God:

> May the words of this prayer be acts of pure love, adoration, thanksgiving, satisfaction, trust, and surrender to your holy Will.

Godly prayer comes from a trustful, loving heart open to the One whom we, lovingly, seek. This is the second mention of 'adoration' reminding us of its importance, for it is the consequence of being afire with love. Adoration places us in a right-relationship with God as we allow our soul to be enfolded in the Trinity. It is a primary Christian act, directing our hearts to that which is not self-serving but creative, loving, merciful and compassionate. It concerns surrendering ourselves to the One who is present in, yet beyond, all things, realising a deep flow of love founded on humility:

> Let this prayer be for my weak self a spiritual communion, an act of humility and of perfect self-denial; and may it be a sacrifice of praise and glory to you, O blessed Trinity. Amen.

We cannot pray aright unless we deny the demands of our ego-driven self and, in this, we're aided by an attitude of praise and thanks as we turn to the great Three-in-One:

> I offer this Office for (*state intention*), to the glory of the Holy and Undivided Trinity and for the salvation of the whole world.

> *Before other Offices:*
> Eternal Father, through the Heart of Jesus, (in union with Mary his mother, St Joseph her husband, *N,*) and all the saints, I humbly offer this holy Office as a sign of love and as a means of reparation. I offer it to the glory of the Holy and Undivided Trinity, for (*here state intention*) and the salvation of the whole world.

As we prepare, we admit to making the offering in a spirit of love and from a desire that all should return to that primal union which God intends. We're to pray *ad majoram Dei gloriam* – to the greater glory of God (and the world's well-being) – guarding against the distractions which affect heart and mind. These can be involuntary, when we find thoughts unconsciously emerging; or voluntary, when we give them our attention (holiday plans, financial concerns, meals, etc. …). In either case, once we recognise what's happening, we need to gently recollect our attention and re-join ourselves into the prayer of Jesus.

The words formed by our lips need to enter the heart; it's there we're to both attend and lovingly hold them so they might be the means whereby our affections help unite us with God. As the *Opening Prayer* in *Daily Prayer* says, we're to 'pray with one heart and mind that the light of God's presence may set our hearts on fire with love'.

SANCTIFICATION OF TIME

IT MAY SEEM odd to consider this as an aspect of prayer but, following Temple practice (and Jewish/Roman tradition) of dividing the day into Hours, the Church adopted specific times for prayer to focus on God's timeless relationship with creation. Just as the sun regularly sets and rises and the seasons of the year come and go with a pattern, enabling and reflecting the cycle of life, so the rhythm of the Office aids growth.

It helps us partake of the activity of the Holy Spirit through time and eternity, building awareness of God's involvement with creation, training us to view life from that divine perspective. Living 'in a constant recollection of the presence of God' means realising the interplay between *chronos* (natural/human time) and *kairos* ('kingdom' or God's time). As the *Daily Office SSF* goes on to say (p. 679):

'In accordance with Jewish tradition, and sanctified by the practice of Christ, the

Christian Church has, from the earliest times, consecrated moments of time so that, through prayer and praise, they become the vehicles of God's time, the time of the sovereignty of God. This has been principally done through the use of two liturgical cycles: firstly of the day, the week and the year, and secondly of the memorial of the Saints.'

The Jerusalem Temple, set in the heart of the Jewish nation, enabled *kairos* to be realised within the Holy of Holies – that place of God's reign which humankind entered in the person of the High Priest. Once this place of encounter was destroyed Christians developed those formal prayers which lie behind the *Liturgy of the Hours* so that, when we pray them, we're connected to an historical and theological river of devotion enfolding creation.

Just as Temple worship reflected aspects of God's activity, so the Office is a means of entering *kairos*, God's dynamic within the context of our ongoing salvation in which we are to live and know ourselves:

'The regular sequence of Hours, or sanctification of time … is given colour and interest and variety and brought into direct relation with the total movement of the Church's liturgical year by the variable antiphons and hymns which adorn it; giving to the psalms and canticles a special emphasis and intention, commemorating the great events of the Christian cycle and heroes of the Christian family; and by the responsories attached to the lessons. Through these enrichments the Office has gradually become a stylised expression of the Church's faith and love, and a devotional commentary upon her life.' [10]

Kairos and *Chronos* are united so that the sanctification of times and seasons reflects the sanctification of creation. This is an insight the church needs to reveal to the world as we engage in a common concern for its well-being. For the heart of creation bears the image of its Creator.

ک

(Whilst what follows is based on the seven-fold Office, its structure and content vary according to specific need, and most Religious Orders have developed their own forms.)

VESPERS/EVENING PRAYER

Vespers (Latin: evening, or evening star) celebrates Christ the Light in the coming darkness. It is the first service of the liturgical day, which may seem odd but follows the biblical account of creation (Genesis 1:5). The 'lighting of lamps', which can take place during the Office, reflects a Jewish affirmation (Exodus 30:8f.) that light has triumphed over darkness. It also recalls the account in Genesis when the first humans entered darkness after being expelled from Paradise, resulting in a long period of preparation as our ancestors sought God's promised Saviour.

As nature begins to settle down for the night, a hymn (the *Phos Hilaron* dating approximately from the second century AD) can be sung whilst candles are lit, especially on Saturday. It causes the heart's eye to turn to him who is scattering the darkness with his radiant light.

Hail, gladdening Light,
of his pure glory poured
who is the immortal Father, heavenly, blest,
holiest of holies, Jesus Christ our Lord.

Now we are come to the sun's hour of rest,
the lights of evening round us shine,
we hymn the Father, Son,
and Holy Spirit divine.

Worthy are you at all times to be sung
with undefilèd tongue,

Son of our God, giver of life, alone:
therefore in all the world your glories,
Lord, they own.

Following this, verses from Psalm 140 may be sung during which (as in the Temple) incense is offered (*cf.* v.2). Then, after the Psalms (which may be introduced and concluded with short antiphons focusing on the season or feast being celebrated), Canticle and Readings the *Magnificat* takes us into Mary's great song of praise. This is also a heart-felt reflection on what the coming of Messiah means for all peoples. We conclude with the Our Father and an appropriate Collect (summing-up prayer).

COMPLINE/NIGHT PRAYER

This short Office is, probably, the most popular of all. Commemorating Christ's entrance into Hades through the darkness of Holy Saturday we ask to depart in peace, the words and structure providing a sense of satisfying completion and fulfilment to the day. Beginning as a (memorised) monastic observation it prepares us for entrance into a time when our sub-conscious takes control, commending us to the care of God through the darkness. It's a powerful tool in settling any anxieties or fears we may have, as one of the readings reminds us: 'Be sober, be vigilant;

because your adversary the devil, as a roaring lion, prowls about, seeking whom he may devour' (1 Peter 5:8). Even if the devil hasn't bothered with horns and hoofs for many years wickedness does prowl around, so we sing:

> From evil dreams defend our sight,
> From fears and terrors of the night;
> Tread under foot our deadly foe,
> That we no sinful thought may know.

Praying the unvarying, traditional psalms (4, 91, 134) can enable them to sink into the heart as we seek God's protection, both through the night and as we prepare for our final rest awaiting the resurrection.

> In peace we will lie down and sleep,
> For you alone, Lord, make us dwell in safety.
>
> (Psalm 4:8)

Finally, it's traditional that before entering the silence of night we conclude by singing one of the beautiful seasonal anthems commending us, in the words of a hymn translated by the Anglican scholar, Athelstan Riley (1858-1949), to 'Jesus' tender Mother'. This can be, for example, the ancient and haunting *Salve Regina* or a Greek Orthodox anthem translated and set to ethereal

music by the (Anglican) Benedictine nuns of
Malling Abbey, Kent:

> Into his joy, the Lord has received you,
> Virgin God-bearer, Mother of Christ,
> You have beheld the King in his beauty,
> Mary, daughter of Israel.
> You have made answer for the creation
> to the redeeming will of God.
> Light, fire and life, divine and immortal,
> Joined to our nature you have brought forth,
> that to the glory of God the Father,
> heaven and earth might be restored.
>
> (*Celebrating Common Prayer*, p. 267)

NIGHT OFFICE/NOCTURNS/VIGILS

Whilst this 'Midnight' Office is, primarily, a
monastic observance it can be a helpful prayer
during sleeplessness. Comprising scriptural
readings and the offering of psalms it was inspired
by Psalm 119:62, 'At midnight I will rise to give
you thanks, because of your righteous judgments',
together with the parable of the Wise and Foolish
Virgins (Matthew 25:1-13). Some see within this
Office the theme of the Hebrews' night-time flight
from Egypt (Exodus 12:31f.).

It also re-connects us with another liberation,
the *Anastasis*, the entrance of Christ into Hades
where he freed our primal ancestors, Adam and

Eve, leading creation from the darkness of death into the new light of life. St Mark of Ephesus (1392-1444) said: 'The beginning of all the hymns and prayers to God is the time of the midnight prayer. For, rising from sleep for it, we signify the transportation from the life of the deceit of darkness to the life which is, according to Christ, free and bright, with which we begin to worship God. For it is written, 'The people who sat in darkness saw a great light." [11]

The general tone of this Office is one of faithful commendation and hopeful expectation and it is still celebrated by many monastics, along with Terce, Sext and None. The latter three terms refer to times of the day (third, sixth and ninth 'Hour'), whilst Midday Prayer (taking their place) is increasingly popular. But the practice of saying Offices one after another, 'to make sure they're said', isn't to be commended: it's an approach from a certain legalism rather than the realisation that these forms of prayer sanctify the Hours for which they are set.

LAUDS/MORNING PRAYER

The next pivotal celebration comes first thing in the morning as nature awakens to worship its Creator and thankful praise is offered in honour of the new day and the dawn resurrection (John 20:1f.). This Office is informed by that longing for the coming of the Messiah found in the Hebrew Scriptures. It takes its name from the psalms of praise (*Lauda*) 148, 149 and 150, traditionally sung after the variable psalms, expressing longing and hope for what the day will bring. These *lauda* psalms also unite our hearts with the praise of awakening creation, renewing our own sense of light and life.

As early as possible that simple statement, 'Lord, open our lips' is prayed helping to consecrate all that will be said not just in the Office but throughout the day (to pray it at other Offices suggests that it is only through their words that we praise God). That is followed by a Canticle, traditionally the *Venite* (*Come* ... Psalm 95) which, if Morning Prayer is not said, is used in the *Introduction* of whichever becomes the first Office of the morning.

Its structure, drawing on a vast treasury of spiritual and human understanding, aids the offering of the self to God at a time when we can still feel tired and in need of being fed. After the hymn, psalms and biblical reading, a further, variable, *canticle* is offered. The greatest of these is, arguably, the (sadly neglected) *Benedicite, omnia opera Domini* (Daniel 3:57f.) traditionally sung during the Sunday and Feast-day psalms. The *Benedictus* (Luke 1:68-79) joins us into the prayer of Zechariah who prophesied, at the birth of his own son, John the Baptist (Christ's herald), that God would 'raise up a mighty saviour' for Israel.

THE LITTLE HOURS

These comprise psalms and prayers offered during the day. Their names come from the times when they are customarily prayed:

- *Terce* The Third Hour (approximately 9 a.m.). The Holy Spirit continues to move through the world as she created God's new People;
- *Sext* The Sixth Hour (Midday). Resting in the middle of the day when the world was shown the Crucified, this Office can involve praying through Psalm119, that reflection on God's Law;
- *None* The Ninth Hour (approximately 3 p.m.). Returning to work as Christ is – unknowingly – taken from the cross.

Prime was the First Hour (6 a.m.) dating from the time of St Benedict, although a form of dawn prayer was known to St John Cassian (360-435 AD) in the Egyptian desert (*Institutes, 3.4*) and is used by the Orthodox. Cassian claims the monks in Bethlehem invented this Office to stop them returning to bed between Lauds and Terce. Together with *Compline*, these Offices form ideal prayers which enable us to enter further into the Mystery we celebrate.

ɞ

The complete Office is a sustained meditation on Christ. Individually they enable us to praise God through salvific moments, for the Hours are created to reflect aspects of the time (*chronos* and *kairos*) when they are prayed. For example the *Benedictus* at Morning Prayer, uttered after Zechariah regained the gift of speech, is appropriate after the speechless night hours. Just as cockcrow heralds a new day so it concerns the one who was to be Christ's herald. It opens us to the mind and heart of one who longed for the coming of the Messiah and a new day for Israel. Similarly the *Magnificat*, at Vespers, takes us unto the heart of Christ's Mother as she prepares to give birth to the true Light of the world. Both are profound meditations, filled with meaning.

ɞ

We all know the importance of a healthy, balanced diet and how eating at irregular intervals or too much, or too little, is dangerous so in a similar way a regular prayer structure aids growth in faith. People sometimes claim they don't have the time for prayer, yet devout Muslims manage five formal daily prayer times. Giving over a set time to the work of God helps determine how we live and involves focusing on God's relationship with the world. Just as the sun sets and rises at regular intervals and the seasons come and go with a pattern enabling and reflecting the cycle of life, so the Offices aid divine growth. They help us partake in the activity of the Holy Spirit and build knowledge of God's activity in all creation, enabling us to view life from that perspective.

SEASONS

LOOKING FURTHER, ONE of the great benefits of the Office is the way it takes us beyond any personal concerns. It lifts us from whatever we may be conscious of and opens the heart's eye to the world in which we're placed *and* that which beckons us. Woven throughout is an awareness of seasons, nature and the cosmos, all of which relates to Christ and work of the Spirit.

> O Trinity of blessed light,,
> O Unity of primal might,
> As now the fiery sun departs;
> So shed your radiance in our hearts.
> > (Evening Prayer, *Hymns for Prayer*
> > *and Praise,* 259)

In the northern hemisphere these reflect and 'dialogue' with the Christian year, uniting us with earth's dynamics. Whether in times of celebration or more mundane but no less important 'Ordinary Time', from the moment we awake to the world's anticipation at the coming of Christ our Light, to the moment we commend all things to the darkness (hiding the presence of God) the Office unites us with the movement of the cosmos.

Just as the passing of nature's seasons aids growth and the interruption of these, or disturbance due to human folly, endangers their life-giving cycle so it is with the Church's Year. By observing the rich content of each Office, we can gradually integrate God's work in creation and salvation with the seasons. This re-connects us with how we once realised the relationship between prayer and the cycle of life. As Autumn, Winter, Spring and Summer enable physical, emotional, and spiritual growth so Advent, Christmas, Lent and Easter, if observed in their fullness, take us into the mystery of creation, redemption, and sanctification. Times of preparation and – often ignored – 'Ordinary Time' mark the way we need periods of patient waiting for human flourishing beneath God's gaze. Praying through the Church's Year enables us to realise how this form of Prayer speaks to life's dynamic in a way self-developed forms may not.

As families, communities and nations observe celebrations recalling their stories and heroes, showing how (for better or worse) they inform us, so birthdays, anniversaries and national memorial events help shape who we are. It's for this reason we celebrate the saints who express life in the timeless Kingdom and invite us to ceaselessly pray, with Mary, 'thy will be done'. Finally, we remember the dead in order to aid them by our prayers.

DAILY DEDICATIONS

Traditionally, each day is dedicated to an aspect of God's activity enabling the week to reflect the whole Paschal Cycle. One such Cycle is:

- Sunday: Light triumphs over darkness in Creation and through the resurrection.
- Monday: The coming of the Holy Spirit.
- Tuesday: Advent hope.
- Wednesday: The Incarnation.
- Thursday: Epiphany, Eucharist, and the Mystery of the whole Church.
- Friday: Passion, cross, death and burial of Christ.
- Saturday: Kingdom of the Saints and Vigil of the Resurrection (with reading of the Sunday gospel at Evening Prayer).

DISCIPLINE

ST PAUL EXPLAINS that those setting out on the Christian way may need to be fed with 'milk' rather than 'solid food' (Ephesians 4:12f.). But to grow we need a substantial diet involving a disciplined life as a means to help that inner-conversion from self to Other-centredness. Being committed to pray the Office at regular intervals aids that as it trains us in the responsibility of having to do certain things whether we feel like it or not, offering a means of re-forming the ego-driven self. It reminds us that some things are good for us even when we don't, consciously, feel their benefits.

According to the Church of England, 'Every clerk in Holy Orders is under obligation, not being let by sickness or some other urgent cause, to say daily the Morning and Evening Prayer, either privately or openly' (Canon C 26). The Second Vatican Council went further urging 'that the chief Hours, especially Vespers, are celebrated in common in church on Sundays and the more solemn feasts. And laity, too, are encouraged to recite the Divine Office, either with the priests, or among themselves, or even individually'. [12]

Some find the notion of 'obligation' difficult, but there's a reason – we have a duty to pray, to be as yeast in the dough or like those seeking treasure buried in a field. With its round of psalms, readings, prayer and praise inherited from the many monastic communities in England at the Reformation, the Office feeds a storehouse within the subconscious. It gradually works on it as gravel carried by a river wears away any rocks over which it passes and has nurtured much of what gives Anglicanism its uniqueness.

Life in a Religious Order showed me that, fundamentally, the Office is the prayer of God's people and not a clerical celebration, so it's helpful if the Officiant presides from amongst the congregation. And whilst it can be prayed anywhere, doing so in the choir (where monastics pray) or a chapel helps sanctify the House of God, showing that it's not just the place where people gather on Sundays.

If prayed in church we're not to be stuck in 'our' places, something I realised in community where, if brothers were absent, we'd move to fill empty spaces because of the importance of realising ourselves as Christ's Body at prayer. Some instruction into praying together is beneficial, especially in pointing out that common prayer is an exercise in the virtue of humility, for we're to make sure that the sound of our voice and the tempo in which we speak doesn't dominate.

If prayed alone it's important (especially for clergy) to have set times: 'I *have* to stop at 6pm to say Evening Prayer – it's advertised so (irritatingly maybe) I must be there.' The fact no one might come can lead to feeling: 'What's the point …? Who's to know …? Who cares …?', yet it always provides a sacramental encounter with the source of Life and, if you give yourself to the exercise, has its rewards.

Some will need to pray the Office whilst travelling, either using a book or appropriate app (e.g. *Daily Prayer* or *Universalis*). If you are praying by Zoom (or its equivalent) listening becomes very important and most find that when more than two are involved only an 'officiant' and one 'respondent' need be heard, whilst others mute themselves – else cacophony erupts!

Those attracted by external stimuli (becoming more difficult to avoid in our image-obsessed, internet-driven culture) may need the discipline of having to attend to a form of prayer which requires the heart's attention and, tested over millennia, the Office has proven to be of lasting value. Whilst the introvert may need to guard against becoming 'lost' in their inner world, the extravert needs to realise how determinative is our inner life, even if we may not be conscious of its power.

Our primary concern must be to develop a right-relationship with God rather than wanting to simply experience the fruits of that relationship – a misleading motive for any devotional act (cf. Luke 17:10). Our loving service of prayer requires an indifference towards the self, its pleasures and, in some ways, its pains. Loving God means accepting the need to sacrifice the ego-driven self along the path to holiness, aided by the grace that comes through prayer. It's a way that has always involved a purgative death to this 'self' that we can be given, in love, to the Other as we desire to live to God's glory.

Canticles and Hymns

Canticles

These provide a further means to meditate on the time, season or saint focussed by the *Antiphon/ Refrain* (e.g. 'Shine on us who dwell in darkness' on Saturday *Benedictus*, drawing attention to the Descent of Christ into Hell – 1 Peter 3:19). Most canticles are taken from scripture though some come from the writings of the holy ones. Those who consider praying with the words of others to be 'mindless repetition' might reflect on the way, for example, that ones such as the *Te Deum* can unleash a torrent of wonder and praise carrying us further than our own prayer could.

Office hymns

The *General Instruction of the Liturgy of the Hours* (Hierarchies of Australia, England and Wales, Ireland, 1974) reminds us that: 'A very ancient tradition gives hymns the place in the Office that they still retain. By their mystical and poetic character, they are specifically designed for God's praise. But they also are an element for the people; in fact more often than the other parts of the Office, the hymns bring out the proper theme of individual Hours or feasts and incline and draw the spirit to a devout celebration. ... Furthermore, the Office hymns are the main poetic element created by the Church' (n.173).

It is now sung after the *Introduction* where it aids the dynamic of time, season or feast. It's an important source of teaching and commentary concerning the celebration and, in a melodic way, aids the beginning of our prayer. In her book, *Worship* (Eagle Pub., 1991, p.87) Evelyn Underhill says they are the medium which carry something numinous; they give eternal reference to the things of time in and through which God speaks to us and are powerful stimulants for the transcendental sense. All this can be especially seen, for example, in the hymns of Advent with their powerful plainsong melodies:

Creator of the stars of night
Thy people's everlasting light,
Jesu, Redeemer, save us all,
And hear thy servants when they call.
(*English Hymnal*, 1)

Both this hymnal and *Hymns for Prayer and Praise* (Canterbury Press, 1996) offer collections of ancient and contemporary hymns for the Church's year. Many were written by the Church Fathers and reveal to us something of their spirituality whilst being carefully crafted expressions of our faith sung to plainsong's sublime beauty.

THE READINGS

EVERY CHRISTIAN NEEDS to read their Bible on a regular basis. Celebrating the daily Office provides an excellent means of encountering those sacred texts which, if we allow them into our heart, will help nourish and (in)form us. Reading scripture in this way engages us with the whole Bible rather than those bits with which we're familiar or have come to like.

We're bathed in it throughout and, in that immersion, encounter Jesus – the Word of God. For this reason, silence after listening to the scriptures will enable what we've heard to settle into our hearts rather than declaring (the obvious) 'Here ends the reading'. After all, the Word is known in silence (Wisdom 18:14f.) so we need to allow silence rather than rushing onto the next thing.

> 'Without silence words become empty'
> (Society of St John the Evangelist,
> *Rule*, Ch. 27).

Some replace the Second Reading from scripture

with one from the Fathers or saints, in which case it's traditional to use an Old Testament/Apocrypha reading at Matins (or one from the New Testament at Vespers) for the former heralds the Son whilst the latter celebrates his enlightening.

Finally, the Office isn't something to be got through before the 'real' work begins as the Franciscan 'Principles' say: 'it is of little value to be present at the common devotions in a formal or careless spirit. [Brothers and sisters] must seek to make of each office an offering of true devotion from the heart' (Day 16).

PRAYERS

IT'S TRADITIONAL TO conclude the Office with litanies of intercession and thanksgiving, the Our Father and a Collect. (As the words 'for thine ...' were not taught by Christ but added by the early Church they're often omitted). Some will follow this with a period of contemplative prayer, Ignatian *Examen* or devotion such as Exposition of the Blessed Sacrament – even if only one person is there. The whole of the Office is a form of intercessory prayer in which all can be held, for it expresses the joys and sorrows, wonders, needs and fears of everyday life. It's not a prelude to lengthy prayers but a means of offering the needs of the living and departed in Christ's prayer. Whatever intercessions are finally offered could conclude with a time for people to share their own, but mustn't overshadow the liturgy.

WHICH FORM TO USE?

RELIGIOUS, WHOSE LIVES are dedicated to prayer, have long realised that Reformation-era liturgies, whilst aesthetically pleasing to some, no longer provide the resource they need. Using services developed at a time of dogmatic dispute cannot mean they are cast in stone – the words need to open windows into God, not become idols. Whatever version is adopted the Office is 'the voice of the Bride herself addressed to her Bridegroom. It is the very prayer which Christ himself together with his Body addresses to the Father.'[13]

The 1662 Book of Common Prayer of the Church of England declares that it is 'repugnant to the Word of God, and the custom of the Primitive Church, to have publick Prayer in the Church, or to minister the Sacraments' in language 'not understood of the people' (*Article 24*). Unfortunately, many today won't understand seventeenth-century English so, when considering which biblical translation (or

Office book) to use, attraction to archaic English, no matter how venerable, mustn't determine choice, for that might easily reduce the power of the word to literary preference.

As the great early twentieth-century traditionalist Anglican poet, T. S. Eliot (who, with C. S. Lewis, had been involved in revisions to the Prayer Book psalter), observed about the passing of time from that earlier century to his and the wonder of fragile, slippery, changing words: yesteryear's belong to another language, today's seem unfamiliar, whilst new ones await a future voice (*Four Quartets*, 'Little Gidding', II.65f.).

Our understanding of scripture, theology and liturgy has also changed over the centuries and because the latter expresses and communicates belief, recent official versions provide a richer, more balanced expression of the faith of the church as they draw on knowledge our forebears did not possess.

With many versions of the Office (and Bible) to choose from, people can wonder which is best. Few can pray all seven so those with busy lives may find two convenient; there will be times when even those must be missed or adapted, and it's important to have a 'holiday' format – possibly one of those readily-available simplified versions. Even if there's not time to pray it all it's important, as a young priest said, to 'do the bits I have time for slowly and attentively, because that's what really matters'. Some use the single-volume *Daily Prayer*, others *The Divine Office* in three volumes finding its traditional, four-fold structure plus Office of Readings richer in content. Others will adopt the Office of their Religious Order and those with less time can find one of the compact editions more convenient.

FINALLY ...

'A quarter of an hour of attention is better than a great many good works. Every time that we really concentrate our attention, we destroy the evil in ourselves.' [14]

Evelyn Underhill makes the point that to be true to our Judeo-Christian heritage worship requires us to retain that 'ancient sense of cloud and darkness, other-worldly fire and light, which still lives in the Psalter; the awe before a sacred mystery which is with us yet never of us, the deep sense of imperfection, and above all the unconquerable trust and the adoring love for God who has set his glory above the heavens and yet is mindful of the children of men' (*Worship*, p.165f.).

Office and Eucharist centre us into life in Christ – the latter with its graceful, sacramental power to transform, and the former providing a reflective means for being enfolded in God's ongoing, saving work. Together they are the means of offering that 'sacrifice of praise', but neither can be a substitute for the prayer of the heart, the daily silent meditation offering a means for the soul's loving abandonment to its Maker. It's important, especially for clergy, to set aside time – say, fifteen or so minutes each day – for meditation/contemplation. Ignoring this risks undermining one's vocation: we need to beware lest love grows cold, in which case our hearts need enflaming again.

All evangelism, pastoral care and liturgical ministry needs to be rooted in conversion of the heart through a loving desire for at-oneness with God. At the Last Supper St John the Divine laid his head on Jesus' breast and became aware of his Beloved's heartbeat, reminding us that prayer is about an intimate relationship with the Lord. Today, as ever, we need to be deepening that relationship not least in order that we can help others on their own faith-journey.

However, whilst the Eucharist has been central to life in Christ since the time of the Desert Elders it has not, necessarily, been celebrated daily whereas the Office has always been the heartbeat of prayer. Having offered it for so long I realise how it reflects Eucharistic living by immersing us in a treasury of creative words, words which nurtured Jesus' Heart through the power of the Holy Spirit, acting as a means of sacrificial offering. To be committed to praying the Office means that the day is being enveloped in prayer: it may not be 'without ceasing' but it's stood the test of time.

'The Daily Office is a sustained act of union with Christ by which we participate in his unceasing offering of love to the Father. In reciting the psalms, singing canticles and hymns, proclaiming the divine word in Scripture, or lifting our voices in prayer, we enter more and more into the mind, heart, and will of Christ, and are borne up by the Spirit in him to the Father.'

(*Rule of the Society of Saint John the Evangelist*, p. 36)

In situations where structures are questioned or collapsing liturgy generally, and the Office in particular, forms part of the scaffolding which holds the enduring truths of our Faith. Just as marriage requires a framework of norms to express the love which, in its early stages, may have flowed easily so prayer requires a structure if it is to grow. We may or may not always 'feel good', but not everything that is good is accompanied by pleasurable feelings, and attentively praying the Office is costly. For minds to wander in prayer may be natural; what matters is our desire, for it is the heart upon which God looks.

Through praying with the words of Jesus we're not just making our requests known but entering the divine narrative, that eternal dynamic desiring the consummation of all things. There's a wide divergence in the way the Office is celebrated by Eastern and Western Christians, and we must beware a legalism leading to judgmentalism, guilt and constriction of the heart. Whilst clergy and Religious are committed to celebrate the Office daily even that is not universal; the guide must be how far, over time, praying it informs, guides and deepens our love of God and neighbour. As 'God's work' it needs to be embraced generously and attentively, and if it begins to feel like a straitjacket, that's something to take to spiritual direction.

> 'The offering of prayer and praise to God in the form of a Daily Office is not primarily a duty to be performed but a liturgy to be celebrated in thanksgiving for the saving acts of God'
>
> (*Daily Office SSF,* 1992, p. 685).

Yet, as one approaches the evening of our days, the need for such structured prayer may lessen (as it will during times of sickness). The attractiveness of spending time with 'centring prayer', such as Francis of Assisi's 'My God and my All', or the Jesus Prayer ('Lord Jesus Christ, Son of God, have mercy on me, a sinner') may gradually move the soul into longing for a simpler, contemplative, silent waiting on the One we love.

ℰ

'The Office ... is an instrument of corporate worship: a device for securing concerted attention to God, and time spent in concerted adoration, subordinating the movements of the individual soul to the majestic rhythm of the Church's liturgical life. But originally it was the Biblical prayer of devout individuals, of the solitaries and the early hermits carrying forward a method of devotion, grounded in the reading of the Scriptures and the saying of the psalms, which was no doubt the daily prayer of the first generation of Jewish Christians and took its general shape and much of its actual material from the synagogue worship in which they had been reared. ... but whether it be recited by individuals in solitude or communities in choir it remains, fundamentally, an ordered method of Biblical worship, communion with God as speaking in scripture and praise of His Name in the Psalms.'

(*Worship*, p. 89)

A M D G

Notes

1. Mother Mary Clare SLG, *Learning to Pray*, Fairacres Publications, 1970, p.1

2. Quoted by Sr. Benedicta Ward SLG, *The Monastic Hours of Prayer*, Fairacres Publs. 178, Oxford, 2018, p.3

3. Ilia Delio, *Simply Bonaventure*, p.54 quoting his *Sentences, d.44,q,1,a.3*, concl.

4. *Corpus Christianorum Latinorum*, vol. 39

5. Evelyn Underhill, *Worship*, Eagle Pubs., 1991, p.76

6. *Sacrosanctum Concilium*, 10, Dicastero per la Comunicazione - Libreria Editrice Vaticana

7. Israel Knohl, *The Sanctuary of Silence: The Priestly Torah and the Holiness School*, Eisenbrauns, 2007

8. Geza Vermes, *Jesus and Temple: Textual and Archaeological Explorations*, Fortress Press, Minneapolis, p.116

9. Hilarin Felder, *The Ideals of Saint Francis of Assisi*, Franciscan Press, 1982, p. 402

10. *Worship*, p.90

11. *Patrologia Graeca* 160, tr. George Dragas, *On the Priesthood and the Holy Eucharist*,

Orthodox Research Inst., 2004, p.48

[12] *Sacrosanctum Concilium,* 100, *sic*

[13] *Sacrosanctum Concilium,* 1174, *sic*

[14] *Simone Weil,* 1951, p.111

OTHER BOOKS BY THE AUTHOR

(published by Canterbury Press)

THE MYSTERY OF FAITH:
Exploring Christian belief
(ISBN: 1786221802)

Concerned with faith formation this book is intended for individuals or groups who want to understand more about the Christian Faith. Written for an 'average' reader it uses the Creed to explore essentials including the nature of the Trinity, prayer, sacraments, worship, etc. Divided into sections it's designed to facilitate group discussion. Foreword by the Bishop of Salisbury. https://canterburypress.hymnsam.co.uk/books/9781786221803/the-mystery-of-faith

WHAT DO YOU SEEK?
Wisdom from the Religious Life
(ISBN: 9781786223456)

This book reveals how Religious Life offers everyone basic wisdom concerning our growth in Christ. It addresses what it means to be human, and how we can live together and will benefit *all* readers and not just those wanting to deepen their faith. Although its focus isn't on promoting the Life, it uses stories concerning various Orders and would be of value to those considering their vocation.

https://canterburypress.hymnsam.co.uk/ books/9781786223456/what-do-you-seek

ENFOLDED IN CHRIST:
The inner life of a priest
(ISBN: 9781786220462)

Inspired by St John Vianney's saying: *'priesthood is the love of the heart of Jesus'*, this book focuses on priestly 'being beneath the role'. It's aimed at clergy, spiritual directors, ordinands and those considering their call, addressing how to develop a healthy spiritual life by drawing on different traditional spiritualities. It suggests cultivating practices and habits to nurture awareness of Christ and foster personal and spiritual well-being.

https://canterburypress.hymnsam.co.uk/ books/9781786220462/enfolded-in-christ

CRUX PAMPHLETS

These concern aspects of faith, worship and the spiritual life and can be downloaded from:
https://johnfrancisfriendship.co.uk/publications